RAVEN'S ECHO

Volume 91

Sun Tracks

An American Indian Literary Series

SERIES EDITOR

Ofelia Zepeda

EDITORIAL COMMITTEE

Larry Evers

Joy Harjo

Geary Hobson

N. Scott Momaday

Irvin Morris

Simon J. Ortiz

Craig Santos Perez

Kate Shanley

Leslie Marmon Silko

Luci Tapahonso

RAVEN'S ECHO

ROBERT DAVIS HOFFMANN

AFTERWORD BY REGINALD DYCK

THE UNIVERSITY OF
ARIZONA PRESS

TUCSON

The University of Arizona Press
www.uapress.arizona.edu

We respectfully acknowledge the University of Arizona is on the land and territories of Indigenous peoples. Today, Arizona is home to twenty-two federally recognized tribes, with Tucson being home to the O'odham and the Yaqui. Committed to diversity and inclusion, the University strives to build sustainable relationships with sovereign Native Nations and Indigenous communities through education offerings, partnerships, and community service.

ISBN-13: 978-0-8165-4471-4 (paperback)
ISBN-13: 978-0-8165-4690-9 (ebook)

Cover design by Leigh McDonald
Cover and interior art by Robert Davis Hoffmann
Designed and typeset by Leigh McDonald in Goudy Modern MT 10-75/14 and Brandon Grotesque (display).

Publication of this book is made possible in part by the proceeds of a permanent endowment created with the assistance of a Challenge Grant from the National Endowment for the Humanities, a federal agency.

Library of Congress Cataloging-in-Publication Data are available at the Library of Congress.

Printed in the United States of America
♾ This paper meets the requirements of ANSI/NISO Z39.48-1992 (Permanence of Paper).

This book is dedicated to the people of my Tsaagweidi clan. They demonstrate to me the principles of perseverance, adaptation, strength, and community. We shall continue to honor our ancestors, our homeland of Skanax (previously known as Saginaw Bay), and our connection to the land and to one another.

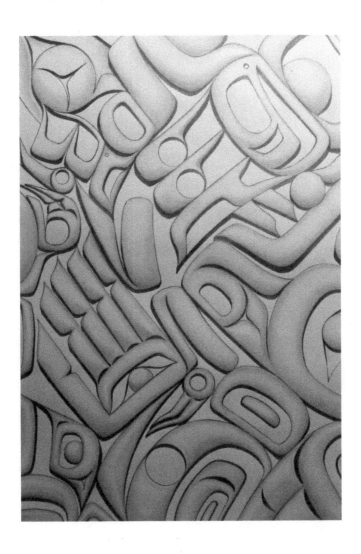

CONTENTS

III

IV

BOOK TWO: RECONSTRUCTION

I

II

III

IV

PREFACE

If I make words, they are Raven's echo. If I move, it is in that rhythm, Raven's heartbeat.

WHEN I WROTE THESE LINES from "Raven Moves," I characterized Raven as an unpredictable and restless Trickster who intervenes in human affairs, often making humans miserable, plagued with fear and uncertainty.

This collection of poems spans different stages of my life. I was twenty-one years old when Raven's Bones Press published *SoulCatcher*. The early poems represent the mental state of an angry, victimized young person. The poems were a way of lashing out, with their anger directed at perceived foes.

In truth, there *is* much injustice that outraged me. In 1869, the United States Army did bomb the village of Kake on Kupreanof Island, my home village, and then burned the rest to the ground. They proceeded to do the same with all the villages on nearby Kuiu Island. Missionaries in Kake persuaded my people to destroy their totems. In my own lifetime, ministers encouraged my people to burn their regalia.

I have to mention the boarding schools because even though I was not subjected to that cruelty, its effects filtered down to me. The purpose of the boarding schools was to enculturate Native Americans to Western society and Christianity. My father attended Sheldon Jackson High School after its boarding school era, but they still punished students for speaking their native tongue. My father did not teach us Tlingit. I believe he was conflicted about whether he should. Our language is now considered endangered. Cultural losses are internal pain passed from one generation to the next, an aspect of intergenerational trauma. I was not aware of this phenomenon as I was experiencing it.

I was fifty-five years old when *Alaska Quarterly Review* published a later set of poems. I had come to terms with many of the things that tormented me earlier. I write with a different conscience. Over the years poetry helped resolve confusion about my cultural identity. My tribal uncle corrected my misperceptions about a father I saw as distant and therefore displeased with me. I found a spiritual way of being that saved me from self-destruction. Poetry allowed me to express my sense of helplessness as progress changed the familiar.

One does not need to be Native American to relate to poetry written by a Native American. All poems have emotions, perceptions, and experiences which are shaped by culture and ethnicity. My poems use Tlingit words and expressions because I want to be true to the way we speak. The same is true of the mentions of Raven, shamans, legends, and place names.

As for my writing process, I wait for ideas to come to me, either in images or words and phrases. They come on their own, in their own time, and sometimes all at once. In writing "Saginaw Bay: I Keep Going Back," I sat down with my typewriter at six in the morning and finished twelve hours later. "Reconstruction" evolved similarly. These urges are simply poems wanting to be born.

How Raven exerts himself in the world changes from the early poems, in which Raven intervenes to make human circumstances more difficult. The implication is that humans become resigned to this discontent, and discontent underlies daily existence. In later writing, Raven is more in the background, an observer. He allows humans to experience the consequences of their own self-destructiveness. Raven is not the root of personal defects, such as insecurity or greed. The later poems reflect this new responsibility and way of being.

Despite the marked change in tone, for many years I had planned to have the original *Soul-Catcher* republished, but was not sure where to start. Instead, I self-published *Village Boy: Poems of Cultural Identity*, poems from both *SoulCatcher* and *Alaska Quarterly Review*. Meanwhile, republication of *SoulCatcher* sat on the back burner.

Then Reginald Dyck contacted me to tell me he thought my poems deserved to be available to a wider audience and offered to pursue republication along with writing an afterword to give context to the poems. Of course I was delighted to see the possibility of this project becoming a reality! He began the arduous task of finding a publisher. Our hope was to find a university-based press so the work could reach a broader audience. I agreed he should write the afterword to provide historical, cultural, and political context of the poems. I could tell from the afterword that Reginald had done extensive research. I am extremely pleased at the insight it provides.

The poems from *SoulCatcher* and *Village Boy* are combined here in this new book and quite a bit of thought was put into how the poems should be organized differently than in *SoulCatcher*.

The original *SoulCatcher* was organized into four sections. Section one addressed prehistory and Raven's involvement in the world. Section two had poems about adapting to a post-contact world. Section three spoke to feelings of betrayal, and section four talked of different types of departure.

In *Raven's Echo*, book I, "SoulCatcher," explores human alienation and spiritual longing. The poems describe struggles to find a place in Tlingit tribal history and contemporary experience. Although many of these poems have a foreboding feeling to them, they also suggest the possibility of spiritual healing.

Book 2, "Reconstruction," suggests different ways of integrating traditional culture into contemporary life. The poems describe our dependence on the land for our subsistence hunting and fishing way of life, and redefining a warrior identity, deciding what to keep and what to discard.

The two books are linked by the common concern of finding a way to live humanely in a world that is historically fractured yet spiritually inviting.

ACKNOWLEDGMENTS

I WISH TO THANK REGINALD DYCK for his commitment to this project of reprinting the original *SoulCatcher* along with poems from *Village Boy*, and for seeing the project through to the end. Thank you for the immensely valuable afterword which provides readers context to the poems, and for the many hours involved in its writing.

In addition, I wish to thank Reginald's wife, Kaori, and my wife, Kris, for their scrupulous proofreading of the manuscript.

Gunalcheesh!

RAVEN'S ECHO

BOOK ONE

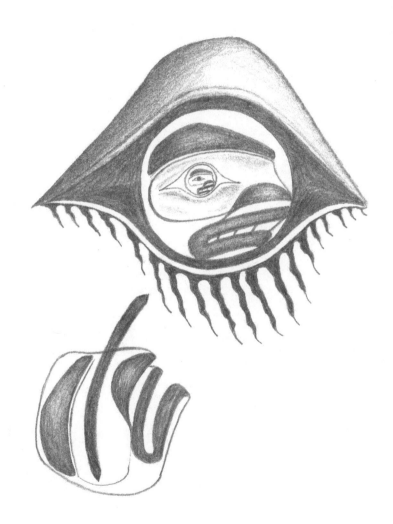

SOULCATCHER

RAVEN TELLS STORIES

Raven, gather us to that dark breast,
call up another filthy legend,
keep us distracted from all this blackness,
sheltered and cloaked by your wing. Answer us
our terror of this place we pretend to belong,
the groping spirits we're hopeless against,
from where all this bleakness keeps rising.
We ask you only to lull us with lies,
expecting the moon to be attached to day
because we're your parasites
nested in feather.
We hope you'll offer
any false hope
we might conjure you back, that when
your mouth opens to tell this,
we will not notice
your tongue black,
your mouth full of shadow.

RAVEN LAUGHS

Raven, you fool us again!
We imagine your graceful glide
braving the way before us. Black angel
who calls us right out of stone,
you fix the world up, prepare our paths.
You spit and form lakes, block the sun;
we find fire you stole. You give all this
and so we dare follow. Little men, middle of nowhere.
Woods all around. You alone are familiar
with the strangeness surrounding.
Our trusted Benefactor, you name us your People,
but turn our backs for a second
and you're off—no footprints to trace.
Signs you leave, we can't figure,
petroglyphs all over. We strain
for that close, betraying cackle,
timidly wait for a huge shadow to fall,
to swallow this ragged lost tribe,
then you swoop up behind
and crap over everyone.

RAVEN ARRIVES

Perched at the doorway of the world
in clusters of branches, tangles of hair,
Raven shit filth-nest
the moment after shell shatter.

Soft-skin dancing blankets,
first feather, big mouth
beaks unhinge
begging for the blackness of your belly.

Ravaging mentor,
they move like you, down
to the very tongue and talon, past
rib, past gut, past violent heart,

first thought
of afterlife—shadows
moving in your shadow, echoes
following your echo.

Newborn death birds
torn from the bramble
fall to earth.

RAVEN MOVES

If I make words, they are Raven's echo.
If I move, it is in that rhythm, Raven's heart,
the air pulsing and rumbling.
It makes me restless.

In the back of my mind,
long-ago night ritual
men crouched in a circle,
drumming the earth.

Raven gets excited,
darts here and there
gathering leaves and bone,
tying all things together
into this dark nest.

Raven's belly swells,
he lifts his wings and buries his head.
The night swirls into itself
and I emerge,
blinking,
a dull thudding in my ears.

SAGINAW BAY

I Keep Going Back

I.

He dazzles you right out of water,
right out of the moon, the sun and fire;
cocksure smooth talker, good looker,
Raven makes a name for himself
up and down the coast from Nass River,
stirs things up.

Hurling the first light, it lodges
in the ceiling of the sky,
everything takes form—
creatures flee to forest animals,
hide in fur. Some choose the sea,
turn to salmon, always escaping.
Those remaining in the light
stand as men, dumb and full of fears.

Raven turns his head and laughs in amazement,
then dives off the landscape,
dividing the air
into moment before and instant after.

He moves north to Kuiu Island, Saginaw Bay—
wind country, rain country,
its voices trying to rise through fog,
the long tongue of the sea
sliding beneath the bay.

Raven is taken by it all:
sticky mudflats, horse clams squirting,
rock pool water bugs skittering,
bulge-eyed bullheads staring through shadow,
incessant drizzle hissing. Oil slick Raven
fixed against the glossy surface of infinity.

II.

The Tsaagweidi clan settled there first;
it was right. Beaches sloped beneath their canoes
greased with seal fat,
canoes that carried the Seal Peoples to these creeks
shaking with humpies and dog salmon.
Everywhere, eyes peered from the woods.
The berries were thick and bursting,
and there were always roots.

They knew how to live,
by the season.

Sometimes it felt like the middle of the world,
mountains circling within reach.

At its mouth on a knoll,
a fortress guarded against intruders.
They came anyway, from the south,
a swift slave raid. They destroyed the village,
the people fled every direction.

A captured shaman was tortured and ridiculed,
his scalp peeled before his very people.
Through blood running in eyes,
he swore revenge
and got it.

After the massacre, the battered clan
collected themselves and moved north
to Kupreanof Island. That became the village
of Kake. That became Kake kwáan.

And, every once in a while,
one sees in his mind
Raven tracks hardened in rock at Saginaw
where Raven dug his feet in
and tugged the mudflats clear into the woods
making a small Nass because he grew homesick there,
and in those moments they feel like going home too.

III.

Kake is The Place of No Rest. It is.

I've heard of men in black robes who came
instructing the heathen natives,
"Outlaw demon shamanism,
do away with potlatch,
pagan ceremony,
totem idolatry.
Get rid of the old ways."
The people listened.

They dynamited the few Kake totems—
mortuary poles fell with bones,
clan identifiers lost in powder,
storytellers blown to pieces
settling on the new boardwalk
running along the beachfront.
Houses are built off the ground now
and my aunt drove the silver spike
in the middle of Silver Street,
sealing the past forever.

People began to move differently, tense.
They began to talk differently, mixed.
Acted ashamed of gunny sacks of k'ínk'
and mayonnaise jars of stink eggs,
and no one mashed blueberries
with salmon eggs anymore.

People walked differently, falling all over.
A storekeeper took artifacts for credit
before his store went up in a blaze.

Grandfather went out in his slow skiff
and cached in the cliffs
his leather wrapped possessions
preserved like a shaman body
that can't be destroyed, that won't burn.

IV.

My grandfather's picture hangs in the church
next to Jesus. He was a great minister. He traveled
with the Salvation Army band, the famous Kake band
called to San Francisco
to play for President Harding.
So that must have been about when?

My father was a young man
when he was sent away with others.
Sheldon Jackson Industrial School, Sitka.
Useful member of society now, they changed him.

Gone from his family years at a time —
one of the conditions.
Punished for speaking his own language.

He graduated,
was sent off to college,
a handsome man,
a lady's man, I heard.
Shy and sad, but likeable.
But goddamn, you had to catch him sober
to know what I even mean.

Now they say I remind them of him.
But you have to catch me sober.

V.

I turn ten or fifteen or something.
Pentilla Logging moves into Saginaw.
Float houses, landing barges and cranes.
Cables to the beach, cables in the woods.
Dozers leave tread marks in mud.

Redneck rejects, tobacco spitters
drink whiskey in rowdy bunkhouses
at the end of day,
brag how many loads, how many turns,
who got maimed,
and did they take it like a man.
Climb all over each other
gawking at the spare women of the camp
and their minds turn to tits and ass.

Some men can't help it,
they take up too much space,
always need more.
They gnaw at the edge of the woods
till the sky once swimming with branches

becomes simply sky, till there is only
a scarred stubble of clearcut
like a head without its scalp of hair.

They hire a few Indians from Kake,
what for I don't know; maybe it looks good,
maybe it's the stories they come with,
maybe it's just they do things so quietly,

even sit speechless
in the stalled speedboat
as high-power rifles chip
at the cliff painting—
the circle around three dashes,
a warning to the people who came
from the south centuries ago,
who destroyed with precision.

VI.

When my uncles were young men,
they crawled on their bellies
through kelp draped rocks
at Halleck Harbor, Saginaw Bay,
at the lowest tide.
They found in the rubble
of boulders from the cave-in,
a hundred skeletons
still in armor and weaponry
piling over each other—
slave hunters
still hunting.

VII.

Because Raven tracks are locked in fossil,
the clam beds snarled in roots,
because we have been told,
we know for a fact
Raven moves in the world.

VIII.

When I was young everyone used Tlingit
and English words at once.
Tlingit fit better.

The old ones tell a better story in Tlingit.
But I forget so much
and a notepad would be obtrusive
and suspicious. I might write a book.
In it, I would tell how we all are pulled
in so many directions,
how our lives are fragmented
with so many gaps.

I know there is a Tlingit name for that bay
that means "Everything Shifted Around"—
what was down there is up here.
I do not remember the name
of the Halleck Harbor shaman
except he was of course most powerful
and I feel somehow tied to him (and was he
the one wrapped in cedar mat,
sunk in the channel,
only to reappear at Pt. White, ascending the beach
to his own grieving ceremony?). I don't know.
I get mixed up. But I know my own name,
it's connected with some battle.

Listen, I'm trying to say something—
always our stories have lived through paintings,
always our stories stayed alive through retelling.

You wonder why sometimes you can't reach me?
I keep going back.
I keep trying to see my life
against all this history,
Raven in the beginning,
hopping about like he just couldn't do enough.

SOULCATCHER

Far from the scent of crackling spruce,
far from throbbing sealskin drum,
into space, into wind,
wild hair flying,
Old Man sings
across the endless dark;
the man who leaves himself
cross-legged, hollow and still.
Medicine Man: SoulCatcher.

In the short, sharp ripples of firelight,
painted carvings and designs
weave and snap
on the bentwood box
holding mystical charms,
soulcatcher amulets
and magic rattle.

Animal people, Ocean people—
this is how he brings them back.
The air begins to move in them.
Thick men in cedar bark clothes.
Incantations, songs, dance, stories.
He could capture your soul if he had to.

The trees know.
They know how easy it is to disappear,
how a figure slouched into fire
now wears a mask
of ash and bone
in a village that still feels air moving.

NAMING THE OLD WOMAN

Why was that old woman
drawing the evening
shadows toward her like a spider?
What were those signs she wove
in dance? She wore a quarter moon
on her face, was wrapped in black
wind and feather, and lugged
a cedar bag of many masks,
many songs that reminded you
of wild animal voices
turning to fog and catching you.

She was carried through the wilderness
of dreams. She was pulled
into the tattooed skin of the earth.
She was the crazy lady
you spent your whole life hunting,
and now, in the smoke,
you rake at the moon shadow
burning the other part of itself
on you, and you can't get her out of you.

DROWNING

We think we are safe
on this beach, in this dream,
luminescence washing the shore.
Low tide odors, sulfur, clams, kelp bed.
We come out of the fog
to cling to this fire
and our own voices
at the edge of the woods,
at the edge of the sea,
somewhere between two kinds of darkness.

I remember stories
of a land where drowning men go,
urged there by Land Otter People,
the Kooshdaakáa.
They take you ashore; they look familiar.
The village itself looks familiar.
Not even surprised at your otter-whistle voice,
you begin to live by your one sense left, hunger.
Scour tidepools for mussels, barnacles,
the flats for clams; you crawl.
Ee! Look at you!
You wouldn't recognize yourself,
hair matted and hanging
over wild, roving eyes,
lips stuck in a grimace.
You stink. You sniff.
Fear comes from you.

Half-awake, waiting for light,
shapes transform. Everything catches our breath.
Listen:
Down there, cockle shells clatter,
a low-pitched whistle
I think is calling.

FRAGMENT OF A LEGEND

Midnight, I'm unasleep.
Low tide moonlight
pulls at the long shore.
The Sea Woman takes me again
in her soft skin
smelling of kelp.

She beaches me
at the original village,
the one
way back there
where all paths
are used by my great ancestors,
rich clans of hemlock.

In their tribal house,
I am guest of honor.
Their gifts:
songs chanted in frail voices
that tell.
Their totems are filled with the wind forever.

MODERN INDIANS

At the mouth of Hamilton Bay, we searched its creeks.
This place some European captain named for himself so
it could exist properly. (Go and subdue the earth, and
name everything in it.) Before the area was logged, they
say you could make out faces blurred in the creek: The
People. Translated, the word Leengít means *The People*.
The People knew their village as Keex'k', The Place of
No Sleep. But everyone fell asleep. When we woke up we
were Tlingits and had the world's tallest totem pole.
Plane after plane, a thousand people poured in
to participate in the pole raising. People sleeping on floors
again. Took a yarder and eight loggers to raise the
damned thing and anchor the cables. A television crew videotaped
the whole shebang. Even the Governor of the State of
Alaska made his appearance—make that one thousand
and one. At the dedication potlatch a self-professed
"Cherokee" did a sundance, and at night everyone got
wonderfully drunk and claimed kinship and babbled
lineage. One day they went home. Kake became Keix
and the Tlingit became Leengít. My sister, Kaaswóot,
(Edna Lucy Davis-Jackson, fiber artist and member of
the Chilkat Weavers Guild, blood quantum one-half Tlingit
Indian), dreamed they took that totem and planted
it at Hamilton Bay, and when they got inside that totem
and climbed to the top, The People looked to the surging
water below and saw hundreds of hands groping, urging
everyone back.

THE ALBINO TLINGIT CARVING FACTORY

We do not take the time hunting
for the perfect grained red cedar
to split planks from with wedge and stone maul.
We do not talk to the trees.
We do not hew and adze
and season our boards. No.
They come from Spenard Builders Supply
on Katlian Street
at $2.75 per board foot.

We do not go to the iron-rich cliffs
for red ocher paint mixed in a stone
paint bowl with dog salmon eggs
spit through mouthful of cedar bark.
Nor do we try for the subdued blue-green
of copper sulphate with virgin's urine,
or black from the deepest charcoal.

You want crude carvings?
You want them harsh and vicious?
Okay,
they might be African for all you care.

Hell, we have to make a living too.

DADDY

Your hand around mine is cold
as you lead me homeward,
passing unpainted houses
with filmy curtains like ghosts
or faded photos in the window.
I know how the inside smells, dried fish.
I know your habits, you whistle
through your teeth miraculously
like north wind through cracked bedroom window
where faces peer at night—
witchcraft, I'm told.
You explain things I'm not ready for,
answer me before I ask
about those other times,
that village all your friends moved to—
Old Timer, Willie, John W. . . .
still hip-booted and plaid-shirted.

Now you, too, come back from there,
from across water,
to bring me stories
in another language.
Your hands weave history
that is not my own, slow and relaxed.
Our eyes are full of each other
and we speak so quietly
I almost don't catch you
retelling my Tlingit name, almost
am unaware of you fading
into deep red evening,
leaving me whistling
something I remember pieces of.

WHAT THE CRYING WOMAN SAW

If all the clocks in the house stopped,
the mirrors still would haunt.
We could not go back
to the past we read in your eyes—
Michigan farm, earth smell following rain,
fresh-mown grass and lilac on the breeze.
Clothes flapping. Woodpile of birch to chop
for the long, frozen winter,
and summer preserved on shelves
under dim basement bulb.

We could neither go back
to a time of fish camps, nor boardwalks
in a small Tlingit village. Smokehouses,
coves of canvas tents. Campfires.
Hand trollers. Salt air and hemlock
and children pulled from school.
Iron pots, sweet red meat, and
everything quietly alive.
A time before cheap whiskey,
we dipped our food in seal oil then.

In our Bureau of Indian Affairs school, there was a full-blooded native teacher,
the first to marry a White woman.
It must have been hard; some things he never talked about.
Did he imagine his dark eyed, brown skinned boy
one day stuck at a typewriter
remembering time two different ways?

AT THE DOOR OF THE NATIVE STUDIES DIRECTOR

In this place years ago,
they educated old language out of you,
put you in line, in uniform, on your own two feet.
They pointed you in the right direction, but
still you squint to that other place,
that country hidden within a country.
You chase bear, deer. You hunt seal. You fish.
This is what you know. This is how you move,
leaving only a trace of yourself.
Each time you come back
you have no way to tell about this.

Years later you meet their qualification—
native scholar.
They give you a job, a corner office.
Now you're instructed to remember
old language, bring back faded legend,
anything that's left.
They keep looking in on you, sideways.

You don't fit here, you no longer fit there.
You got sick. They still talk of it,
the cheap wine on your breath
as you utter in restless sleep
what I sketch at your bedside.

Tonight, Father, I wrap you in a different blanket,
the dances come easier, I carve them for you.
This way you move through me.

I come to tell now, the moving men
are emptying your office.
Everyone thought I would take your place
but as I turn in your dark chair
I recall a night
you tossed in dream
on breath-waves that break
pebbly shores of canoes,
where fog people move
in the old Tlingit village
among your smokey clan house
and an emerging totem, a woman
I remember as Grandmother
gesturing, talking words almost familiar.

Your sleep speech grows gutteral
and I feel something pull
that, when you wake, I want to ask you about.

BLACK BUOY

I dreamed it rose
giant against the islands
of graves.

I dreamed we approached
alone, hands outstretched.

We felt its hollowness,
we were impressed,
we were intimidated.

The sea was there;
it was ancient.

And I wondered,
would we ever
drift back
to our village growing small?

OUTGROWING OURSELVES

Say we build a cabin ourselves, right down
to the very doors and windows, way back
there in the woods because we choose solitude.
Hang Indian baskets and paintings and
carvings and masks inside and
line the shelves with poetry and sentimental
knick-knacks and photo albums.
Put the bed I built over there by the door
so we can kick it open mornings
to listen to birds and wind. Use the bed
for a couch, always keep it filled.
Take that cat, that dog there and
keep one on the porch to yap all night;
the other to purr by the stove, curled
like it could live this way forever.
Go down to the stream for dishwater,
don't sneak any of those beers, I'll be watching
from this rocker on the porch.
Plant a strawberry garden on the side,
a wild one, and a grass garden in the front.
Now stand back and see that it is good.
Leave the doors open by accident one day
and have bug carriers and mice and
spiders drive us into panic.
Every weekend let us lie naked, outstretched
on the woodshed and let hemlock needles
find our ribs.
Watch with half-open eyes, the smoke snaking
lazily around this clearing.
Listen how the raven has three echoes:
one from the swamp, one from the woods,

and one from its own throat.
And tell me how you don't look forward to winter.
Tell me how I need to get a respectable job
so we could get off the food stamps and canned
fish and jarred berries, so we could get electricity,
so we could get a radio, so we could get a CB,
so we could get a TV, so we could get a stereo, so
we could get a vacuum cleaner, so we could
get a microwave oven, so we could get a truck,
so we could get the hell out of here.
Decide to go to college in a year or two
so we could learn we don't know proper things,
so we could seek lovers to show us how little
we have together, so we could pack our separate
bags and prepare for the good life.

THE INDIAN GIVER CALLED DEATH

This little poem is so evil
it doesn't even need the word "death" in it
but you find it here anyway: death.

How many times I have offered it,
this death poem.
How many times I have watched you
tear into it, rip it apart,
trying to get to its greedy black heart
to wear it close to your breast.

You come to me at night
and when morning arrives
we find ourselves
still craving darkness
and you begin licking
remnants of it
lingering on my lips.

THE INHABITANT

The dream pushes into me
like an odd-shaped bone
trying to fit.

It breaks my rib,
and, removing it,
shoves bluntly into place.

I am this dream,
I am this bone, this rib,
I make into a loon
and name it "self"
and give it glass wings to break.

It is I
who sink with the sun
to dive for blood pearls
to sew on my back for you.

It is I
who decide to hug a rock
to my chest
and never let go.

FERTILITY RITE

You make your rounds again,
those full moons in your eyes
always tugging at my seas of blood.

You open your arms and draw me
onto your shores
and I drift into your skin.
You lock me in; this is
my asylum.

We throw ourselves
into the moon
and thrash and turn
our heads
from side to side
like suffocating fish.

The tides swell in our rivers
till they're gorged as kelp bulbs.
Two tidal waves collide
and leave us barely
sensing we have drowned
and now float
in lunar emptiness.

We sink
behind our darkening eyes
and survey the damage.

THE MAN WHO LOVED KNOTS

Evenings, your back is thick with blood
where the sun has flogged you,
black pools appear at your feet.

You step into them
with your baggage
full of bones,
knowing they are required
on this exodus.

As you slide downward
and find a perfect fit,
you close the skin
over your head
and I begin to sew
the sutures you once showed me.

GAME

I am a small boy again
and Father wraps me in deerskin
and tells me to sleep
as they sit by the fire
boasting endless tales of hunting.

        My father, once upon a time,
        shot an out of season deer,
        dragged it, kicking, into a thicket
        of brush, and smashed its skull with rocks.
        That deer wouldn't die, it just
        hung out its tongue, rolled up
        its eyes and
        bleated and
        bleated.

I dream of toy animals
you squeeze and they cry,
of hysterical children mutilating them.
I'm jolted awake to a rifle-crack.
I try to sit up
but only a deer cry
bleeds from my throat
and the men sit around
laughing and elbowing each other.

ARCHEOLOGY

Like every man,
my face carries its scars.

Like every man
whose prospective curator
descends the caverns of dreams
etched in his skull,
I allowed myself to be unlocked
and found my treasures plundered.

Like some men do,
I barricade the entrance
and keep a fire
fueled with body parts
unearthed in me
to blacken the cave walls with soot.

The excavation continues
day and night;
I hollow myself.
I chip the last fragments away,
break through to this crowd
you wait anxiously among,
speechless, aghast.

EVICTION

This dark orchard,
and the shadows of myself,
and the shadows you wipe from your lips,
and you smiling uncertainly,
on the verge of your evil dream;
it was the perfect illusion
till you started seeping from yourself,
and I strangled you to keep you in,
and watched you slide through my fingers.

IV

FASTING FOR EIGHT DAYS

Do you want that here?
Out here in the woods,
cedar spruce and hemlock
persuade you to shed clothing

that you may embrace them
as long-lost brothers
to translate their whispers
of a song that rises through roots,

the sigh of rock
wearing down to cold streams,
carried to seaweed shores

where you bathe in salt breeze
and stare
right in the face of
rock mountains
breathing blue light.

CHANGE OF SEASON

I am uncivilized
because I choose to live.

Once when I was younger,
I was a student of biology.
We split the hemispheres
of the brain and spoke
in Latin terms
of organs and nerves.
I had to leave school to be educated.
I had to lose my mother and father
in order to find them.

This was my impulse:

> to bury compass and watch
> in the gut of the earth
> and wander the wilderness,
> finding how to hunt as a man
> and why I must.

The sky was crossed with geese forty times,
then I came back,
my speech lost in blood.

INTO THE FOREST

Here, heavy boughs hang
with strands of withes
and wispy goats' beard fungus
takes the place of sky.

So dim and mystical,
I hear legends whispered
from way back
behind each tree, each cedar
straining toward totem,
the bark skin twisting and unwrapping
exposes bold formlines curing
to knots like whorls on fingers.
Grain takes off into branches, and beyond
imagination.

Everything rises
from mere roots anchored in the brown
bone of the earth. Beneath the moss,
a mute voice begging for voice.
A carver, I listen with hands.
Forest creatures hesitate,
all senses wide open.

TAKING THE NIGHT TRAIL

This is the kind
of night when
the moist forest shadows
lift themselves, spread
and offer their fingers.

The moon roams
the treetops,
you shade your eyes.

A tree falls from its roots,
stretching silently
into itself.

If your feet begin
to fade on the way,
you're so much closer to home.

HOME

On the shadowed side of moss,
your wrinkled fingers trace
a submerged trail of roots
and shallow caverns
for worms' nests,
trickle without sound.
You lie cold—
This all closes in on you.

RAVEN IS TWO-FACED

Raven eyes blink
    day / night   day / night . . .

The world has its top,
its underside, and
Raven tracks lead everywhere.
You can tell he's been busy.
Shifty. That he's got this game
of intrigue down, because
he's made certain everything
about him has two sides.

There's no way out;
you can turn this poem
inside out,
trying to interpret
its other meaning.

RAVEN DANCES

Any other time you'd have dismissed it
without a second thought;
a dead, lingering day,
edgy flock of ravens
shuffling, impatient as always.
You never know what they're up to anyway.
But there is this child,
wildly waving his arms.
Ravens nod. The child dances and screams.
Nearing this performance
you note his back is feathered,
black lines run down his cheeks
and he hops and glances about.
Ravens flash in his eyes,
beat him to the ground. You hear a crunch
of shattered skull,
and, in that instant,
black shadows escape,
leave you with this fragile form,
a small human dance rattle.
You withdraw and find
your head, too, is full,
with raven wings beating.

BOOK TWO

RECONSTRUCTION

VILLAGE BOY

He was Village Boy. Years later, he's Village Boy.
Keex' kwáan. Kake people. Aa.a.
Didn't talk much then.
Still doesn't.
His high school year, they moved to the city.
He was dumb in school.
Dumb Village Boy!
Oh, he was so ashamed . . .
Ashamed of who he was, where he was from.
There were names for people like him.
He made himself thin,
missing everyone between classes.
I studied him like a foreign language.
Waiting all day for the end of day
when Carving came.

At the end of day is when I saw Village Boy's designs,
when he finally took out his hands.
"Killer whales!" he told me, making his arm a fin slicing waves.

Carving Teacher went to school with Charlie Pride.
He was really Shop Teacher, no Native teachers then.
Carving Teacher drops his jaw,
"By golly, sure looks like Kwaktootle art there, Bob!"
Village Boys head turns,
"You talk funny. And I can't carve."

Carving came to them, like it had to, both of them.
It fixed everything. Kept him from slipping.
They put together the first bentwood box with dovetail joints.
Pretty good! How the carvings made his designs swim!

School dismissed. Village Boy went home.
He finally went home.
Village Boy said, goodbye. Carving Teacher said, thank you.

The way this story goes, decades later
Village Boy sits with Carving Teacher's grandson.
Shows Grandson his cuts.
Now Village Boy's eyes flood with thanks
when Grandson leaves.

The things we need come when we need them most.
If you took away our knives
our hands would be just fists.

HE WAS A DANCER

He was a dancer. All over the floor.
The bed of hemlock that was the ocean.
He rode it. Swimming through the air
with fists of feathers.
Seventy years and still lithe.
I wanted to move like him,
bare feet coming down exactly
to the skin tight drum.
Cawing like Raven.

He had long, silver hair
that whipped and kept
your eyes from stopping
on the old dance blanket.
I wonder where he kept it hidden, his only property—
his shack by the humpy creek?
The smokehouse after the fire?
It was a hard life for him after his wife died.
He made his rounds at just the right time.
Returning home with gunny sacks of canned goods
tossed over his shoulder.

He was a dancer,
wool and sweat.
He died drunk, sprawled with no blanket
in a fire-gutted house.
Indian village, Sitka, 1975.
No teeth, almost deaf.
Death grip on wine jug.

Once again
somewhere,
he makes the rattle sing,
sealskin, ermine headdress, button blanket
unfolding themselves.

Once again
somewhere,
the singers recapture their notes,
their persistent songs
pulsing with the diving figure,
his arms outstretched.

BLIND MAN

The old man rocked on the rickety porch,
staring behind dark black glasses.
He always faced the water,
as if it were telling him something.
He lived in a little world, everything within reach.

Blind Man could sample a tray of seaweeds and name the rocks they came from.
In his day, every point of land had a name, every cliff, even big rocks.
You memorized these things, you spoke to the places because they kept you alive.
He never got it wrong; it was more than taste.

We played a game,
creeping under the stairs to tug a pant leg.
He did not lurch. Never smiled, never got angry.
Just rocked. And stared.
We weren't trying to be mean; we were village kids.

Becoming men, we feel something strange
curling like smoke that has to come from somewhere—
anger and cruelty just below the surface
coming from a place
we could not see,
that we had no names for.
We're people familiar with the outside world.

We want to hunt and gather for ourselves,
we hunger for delicacies dipped in seal grease,
But rendering fat draws company
insisting on the same generosity as the sea.
We talk guns and horsepower now.
Numbers are everything now.

Another time
it would have been clearer
that the sources of sustenance
have more to do
with the taste of seaweed and the place of its harvest.

WARRIORS

The new warriors battle full court press
in the courts of the ANB Halls.
A framed photograph near the concessions
shows early heroes
dressed for convention;
in this corner,
smart young natives
resolved
to make gains
for a new generation.
The brass placard lists each of them.

Hanging nearby
the Hall of Fame lineup,
you can hear the roar
coming from the stands.

It is carried
by its own power
beyond the walls
into corporate offices
where secret societies
shuffle paper,
dividing the spoils,
pleased that the crowd gets their money's worth.

Raven said—
thinking back to the beginning of the world
when he smudged shit on Ganook, Keeper of Water,
and he lost his guard,
losing exclusive claim
to all the water of the world—

"If you trick someone,
you don't even have to fight."

ROCK OF AGES

On his way to town, the stumbling man passes the tennis court,
drawn to the petroglyph rock heaved upward from buried tide flats.
Something calls him back.
At first, he guessed it was the signs chiseled in stone.
Signs he found one day in some accidental light.

Someone told him it was a calendar.
Those signs tracked time maybe,
mapped old worlds maybe,
recorded sea monsters thrashing, half-men grunting.

The drunk hears these things,
shaking fingers tracing ridges and valleys, circles inside circles.
It became a habit.

The Tlingit tell of floods that covered the earth,
of starting all over,
of rivers that led them under ice sheets down Pacific tidelands.

On the other side of the rock, in that raw land,
a lone man in bear hide
strikes stone on stone . . .
making coherent the vast distance they came.

I've seen him return. Over and over, roaming those ages.
He shifts from foot to foot in winter's slush,
depending on the rock for balance.
He navigates geological eras.
He follows a far-off-yet-not-far-off crunch of feet in snow—
a small band of furry men, staggering across Asia. Just hunting.
There was a bridge between those worlds,
the tracks of woolly mammoth trudging homeward.

I watched this curious bruised drunk, ear to stone, eyes filling up.
His hands on their own, making circles in the air.
The rock sings to him, swollen with history;
impaired enough to simply see
if DNA from petroglyphs were even possible,
at some point upright man would emerge!
This drunk has felt the blood of ancestors,
the ancient procession, the higher laws—
beyond libraries, beyond tectonics, magma and fossil.

Men parked in uniforms see something wrong,
demand of this drunk the nature of his business.
"Simply following the law, keeping my balance, being upright."
The uniform spins his fingers to his temple,
dismissing the shameless drunk,
"Son, you've got rocks in your head."
Tire tracks disappear.

GLOBAL WARMING

September in Barrow, my wife anticipates polar bear,
huge white forms humping across ice fields.
But the ice is rotten and refuses the bears,
according to the elderly Eskimo woman
smiling at the tourist in the tropical palms
some prankster fashioned from baleen of whale
and planted like an absurd Stonehenge.
The old woman swears there were great footprints,
that my wife should find a big stick, then
shrinks on the back of a 4-wheeler
headed for town,
where all kinds of people come
to be on top of the world.

Back in the Alexander Archipelago,
our garden spent
the entire summer
struggling to push out any color
to break the monotonous cold gray
drizzle, a steady sheet
we look through like the plastic
flapping over our windows.
The climate will turn
these failed flowers
into a garden of its own,
one that can survive a drowning island
we look for relief from.

From the hacienda window,
we can almost shake hands
with Mazatlán, its spectrum of colors.
It is so clear and bright
we shade our eyes,
searching for whales that drift like logs from Alaska.
In September, the inland desert is green and flourishing.
In the hills, perhaps a farmer looks down on the resort,
past his coveted agave. In the shimmering city, perhaps senoritas twirl
bright skirts to mariachi trumpets for careless tourists.
We could almost live here, we agree,
the cold air blasting into our room.
The pipes knocking
as though even water needs permission to enter.

SEATTLE BLUES

Yesterday morning, on waking,
I thought I was gazing at a shimmering creek bed,
shadow and sunlight swirling over rocks.
But it was the cherry tree
dancing on the stark wall
with its resident starlings
lifting themselves to the ripest fruit,
the hardest to reach.

Every moment has its details,
every place requires adaptation.
Downtown, studied gentlemen in the secret café
trade the best words
for the chicken parmigiana and strong espresso.
Their discussion covers good literature
between mouthfuls.

Golden Garden Park in the evening—
diners find the boathouse popular,
trains pound northward though plate glass;
right below,
flush men caress hulls in the boatyard.
Out of sight
fishers are propped with lines
hoping the surf gives something for the effort.

When I tire of this district,
I put myself back at my creek,
my home in the woods of old-growth,
a place still unpopular,
small creatures undisturbed at its banks,
feeding themselves with anything good they can find.

DANGER POINT, BAINBRIDGE ISLAND

You lead me into approaching night,
down to eelgrass reefs,
leave behind safe house lights.

Channel marker's strobes
punctuate our thoughts.

Between each pulse,
the red lid of the sky
slowly closes, blinks.
Then we, like irritating specks,
are suddenly gone.

All that remains:
a deepening trail,
naked footprints
close together
in the mudflats at Danger Point.

Afterimage of bone-colored moon
shaken from its mooring
by waves folding over and over.

I make out my voice
going on about the painters, the poets,
derelicts who straggled all the way to death.
About the channel markers,
all the intrepid seamen
who have vanished just-like-that.

Now the odor of seaweed begins to rise.
Now the madrones reclaim all light.

A cry from the invisible sea bird
echoes off the wall of darkness.

This is the point
the sea draws up on either side.
At this point, time hangs momentarily,
then surges around you.
This is any time,

the point where I start to whisper
how this feels all too familiar,
that we might turn back now,
while the tracks that led us here
are still recognizable
as our own.

DIVISION

The geodetic map's accurate
quadrants make plain
the plots that cut the tribal houses apart.
The clansman accepts his lot.

Surveyors diagram invisible lines like intent palm readers.
They turn the men to grains way down there
by the red ink.
You can see them drifting and settling,
making their own kind of sense.

Guide yourself over that topography
the primal woodland, the forest people—that world, yes.
The fire pit children dance against adzed walls.
The house is like a Cedar box preserving precious at.oow—sacred clan treasures—
even as you watch it splinter.

Disgruntled Raven shakes his rattle,
scrambles for the smoke hole
that turned him black, that once breathed and exhaled.
You hear his feet starting to stomp?
His pounding, steadfast feet draw on the earth,
even, then uneven,
even, then uneven.
By HIS dance the land is shaped,
by HIS dance the world is arranged.

THAT river of feet hastens mapmakers' scratchings,
where lines are drawn,
how dissection determines the destiny
of pursuant land holders

wanting, wanting
to claim new life.

Shhh! Down there, wrinkled auntie crouches.
She harvests sweet cloudberries in spruce root basket,
so deep in the bushes
they blot out completely
the increasing storm of agents
demanding the exact amount of blood in her body.

KAKE TOWNSITE SURVEY 3851

Last summer, the swainson's thrush
sang its final notes.
I was saying goodbye to our lot in the woods.

The last light of summer
drifted down like dust
through the old hemlock
on every side of me.

In your startling absence,
I cup the space in front of me,
trying to believe it were just a fragile insect
confused about where to land,
that my hands aren't desperate.

They said I'd get used to it.
But the flies exhaust me!
There's so much silence . . .
Beetles chew on the cottonwood.
Leaves crash at my feet.
Even the dust settling
makes its own little breath.

Labrador tea used to calm me,
the moss used to comfort me.
Now I hear it colonizing the forest
as I wait in my shack
in the woods—
no longer simple woods,
in this misnamed silence
that keeps opening to more silence,
that will soon crescendo.

MONSTER

In mythological time, at Auk Village, there lived a monster—
a sea monster, Gunakadeit, part-wolf, part-whale.
Carcasses piled up behind the village.

A mother's "good-for-nothing" son-in-law trapped the monster, took his skin.
In the dark, wrapped in the ocean, he wears the skin of Gunakadeit.
Good-for-nothing did his deeds.
Beaches turned to fresh meat for that hungry village.

The mother-in-law took the credit. Her people believed they owed her their lives.
To prove her power, she increased her demands, commanding the sea to surrender.
To prove his worth, the son hunted harder.

He should have been done before daylight,
out of the skin before Raven cried. It was impossible.
Dragging himself ashore, half-in, half-out, part-monster . . .
to win favor did him in.
The woman's shame brought her end
when the people put it together.

In real time,
a boy came into the world
birth marked burgundy red, like dog salmon,
foot to head.
When life slapped its first breath into him,
the hands on him stayed hidden.

People were mean.
In the company of men,
his bruises were hidden,
the wine covered it up.
In the dark,

the hands disappeared.
When the heaving monster thrust,
even the ocean shuddered,
his blood sounding like waves.

That's when Dog Salmon Boy fled to the land of stories,
the land of Gunakadeit.
The stories saved him, as stories will.
As stories restore the powerless.

LEVELING GRAVE ISLAND

Some of the arms flew
up to where legs belong. Some
thighs smashed to ribs.
A few skulls smiled into their own pelvis.

Not a hundred years ago,
the placement of bones, each particular
stance, was the position for entering death country.
Broken knees and elbows to fit to chests
were placed on the platform
that floated back to earth evenly in time.

Bodies churn and roil in the earth.
The giant spruce, the eagle trees—
the points of reference go up in smoke.
Nothing is so random.
We lose our direction.
I watch this destruction daily.

Grave markers donated to museums.
Trees explode.
The dozer that was ferried across
has leveled the entire island.
The living destroy the dead,
as the dead claim the living,
like going off in the distance,
growing smaller and vanishing,
like rituals without origins,
like this island that never was and always will be.

IV

TO DRAW MY HAND

In my study, a mirror hangs on the door,
glass etched with praying hands;
in the center, a hole trembles and bleeds.

I wanted to draw them in vermilion ink.
I wanted to draw them Tlingit-style, something that graceful—
that familiar.

If I can draw my hands like that,
eccentric ovoid palms, fingers pressed,
tipped with waxy feathers
that will not fall apart.

My model is not innocent.
It needs to confess
its trespasses, who it has taken from,
where it's been,
what things it has signed away;
it wants to apologize for itself.
Hands cannot hide their guilt.

The ambivalent hand holds the pen,
no longer looking like it belongs to me.

CARVING

Kaashaan, old man, master carver—
perched on alder chopping block,
a sleek killer whale dives in his palm.
Slice, chip, gouge, flick . . .
pungent cedar escapes.

"My tools stay sharp this way, just from use," Kaashaan explains.
Is he playing with me? I can't tell.

He puffs into the blowhole,
cedar shavings spray.
Pointing with the tip of his knife, he tells me
the importance of design—the overlapping formline,
how the central ovoid repeats itself.
At his feet, haphazard curled spirals,
circles, and intermittent commas form,
like some kind of calligraphy,
or magical equation.

The carver leans toward me, "Does the wind around raven sculpt raven,
or does raven sculpt the wind around himself? Do the tide flats emerge,
or is that Tide Woman pulling back her blanket? What matters
is not what's left to the eye, but what's taken away."

That mistake, that little slip I made yesterday, good or bad, is what I'm left with now:
Kaashaan swimming in my head, casting out
my urgent thoughts of the day.
I can't listen too long to Kashaan without getting lost.
I don't tell him.
What we omit, sometimes, is of the same consequence as what's brought out.

RECONSTRUCTION

(For Uncle Topsy, Shaayaxdu.eesh—Tsaagweidi)

I thought my life was in layers
like a complex Chilkat Blanket's warps and wefts:
foreground, background, the native, the not-native.
It couldn't unravel.
My father thought Tlingit but spoke English.
I always heard we live in two worlds,

heard that we learn who we are
by living right with the land,
that it should feed us like mother with milk.
I never hunted, could not speak the language of the forest.
Never fished, could not dance with the river.

To make sense of this place,
I tried to reduce it: mudflats here, cliffs there, clouds above,
sulfur, rock, evaporation—but for all the details
it could not come to life, had no spirit.
I puzzled over this.

I heard we learn who we are by being warriors.
Trained myself to be angry, to be at war.
On my head, a fierce killer whale helmet with a fin that slashes.
Water roiling and adversaries came out of nowhere,
Like Naatseelanei's killer whales seeking vengeance.

Uncle was different:
He wore tubes that fed him oxygen, the summer I lived with him.

One July day when the water was smooth,

we took our uncle to the sockeye stream.
It was all over the CB, we were so proud to get him out.
We brought his air.

We pulled in fat halibut. There was so much!
We thought we fished good! But the fish came to us, Uncle Topsy said.

Gliding across the strait, we took Uncle to Skanax, Saginaw Bay,
ancestral homeland of our Tsaagweidi Killer Whale clan.
We sat there, the boat hardly rocked.
A whale broke the water at the base of our last fort, that stood far above us.
Topsy held out his arms reciting the names, even the people;

where Raven danced, and flirted, and played—
where canoes arrived and were greeted. Or destroyed;
how things that seem mythical, unfolded here—right here!
I felt it. We all did.

And we understood
we didn't bring Uncle here,
he was bringing us here, home.
I thought I needed his memories, his life.
But he told me,
"You know, even when you know the answers, listen. Just listen."
He said my uncle told him that.

He was showing me the way to be human.

Played me the tape of our last real leader.
He was listing the qualities of a worthy chief:
"Your people should always see smoke
drifting from the smoke hole."
The voice was calm and sweet like water. It was satisfying. In Tlingit.

He played its length and studied me, "Did you hear it? Did you hear?"
I said, "But it was in Tlingit."

He pointed to his heart.
In my teacher's presence I felt so safe, like sitting at the fire pit.

I would have to design the dance staff to tell our story.
our story, Tsaagweidi!

I struggled with it for nights,
pinning worn out photos to the clothesline I strung:
the Kake dancers, their drums, their paint, elders long gone, old regalia, old Kake.
They were fading.
I wanted it. I wanted it to come back;
for Topsy's memories to be my memories.

So I played the songs, I turned it REAL LOUD
till the house itself sang, till the photos began to dance and sway,
till the designs came on their own—just like the sockeye in July,
just like the whale met us at Skanax.

I saw it like it was floating in front of me!
Two killer whales, two houses.

There were two killer whales but joined by a single tail
and seals in the body, Tsaa!
It's like that, connected, not disjointed.

When Topsy came from the hospital, I wanted to be the man he described.
I confessed that's not me.
He put his hand on my heart: "You just have to listen, nephew.
It will all come to you, if you stop fighting so hard. It will."

AFTERWORD

Raven's Echo as Reconstruction Project

Reginald Dyck

ROBERT DAVIS HOFFMANN, A "NEO-TRADITIONAL artist/storyteller," calls on humans to nurture both material and spiritual life. In his poems the speaker often feels cut off from Tlingit tradition because of "outside forces: relentless change, government subordination, painful acculturation, and assimilation. . . ." Yet these are not the only challenges his poetry engages. Spiritual connections are also complex and illusive, as Raven here teaches. *Raven's Echo* takes up the question of an individual's position within the universe and within history, including mythic history. These poems offer an imaginative cast of characters, including the playful trickster Raven, who can also be deeply disturbing. Hoffmann's penetrating depictions of contemporary Native life in Southeast Alaska are also troubling. Rather than providing readers reassuring clichés, his poetry offers experiential insights.

The two books of *Raven's Echo* are linked by the common concern of how to live meaningfully and responsibly both materially and spiritually. Book I focuses on efforts to heal spiritual relations within history. Raven haunts the speaker's consciousness. As the subtitle of the key poem "Saginaw Bay" states, "I keep going back." The speaker in book 2, who is more experientially direct, has accepted this commitment to go back. He now struggles to find the right way to reconstruct a life within Tlingit tradition and history. He wrestles with the contradiction between what he has heard—Tlingit traditions—and what he experiences in contemporary life. The poems in this book often tell stories which are less about Raven and more about living in a world of guns and horsepower, global warming, cops, and drunks—although Raven always lurks in the background. The two books are linked by the concern of finding a way to live humanely in a world that is historically fractured yet spiritually enticing.

❋

Book I explores human alienation and spiritual longing. The opening four Raven poems challenge common assumptions about Native religious experiences. Raven baffles, is often not present when needed, destroys as much as he creates, and yet is enticing. "Saginaw Bay" then weaves the history of Hoffmann's Tsaagweidi clan, beginning with Raven recklessly creating the world. This restless, searching poem presents the speaker's effort to find his place in a Tlingit community's past and present life. Because "they knew how to live, / by the season," a good world had come into being through Raven's seemingly haphazard construction job. Yet this did not last.

Hoffmann explains that "Saginaw Bay" is about material loss and spiritual alienation as a consequence of colonialism. Now, only "every once in a while / one sees in his mind / Raven tracks. . . ." Still, the restless, creative energy of Raven finds a place in the speaker as he searches for understanding that can help repair the fragmented contemporary world. In spite of the sense of loss, the speaker picks through the ruins and finds connections with the past. But Raven is always moving, "hopping about like he just couldn't do enough." The speaker finds no final answers.

Book I shifts between the mythic and the contemporary as the speaker explores the possibilities and problems of finding spiritual healing within challenging material and spiritual conditions. This book's concluding section first depicts the speaker's attempt to create a proper connection to nature. In "Fasting for Eight Days,"

> cedar spruce and hemlock
> persuade you to shed clothing
>
> that you may embrace them
> as long lost brothers.

The result is a powerful, mystical experience:

> where you bathe in salt breeze
> and stare
> right in the face of
> rock mountains
> breathing blue light.

The direct language, the staccato rhythms, and the emphatic assonance, alliteration, and rhyme all give an urgent quality to this spiritual apprehension.

Four poems follow in this vein, and then the section makes an abrupt shift by acknowledging that material/spiritual connections are not so simple. "Raven Is Two-Faced" asserts that nature is filled with ambiguities: "Raven tracks lead everywhere. / . . . / he's made certain everything / about him has two sides." Raven is difficult to both apprehend and comprehend.

Book I concludes with "Raven Dances," which describes a child dancing himself into a raven:

> Ravens flash in his eyes,
> beat him to the ground. You hear a crunch
> of shattered skull
> and, in that instant,
> black shadows escape.

This ceremonial experience is as terrifying as it is engaging. The speaker is engulfed by the mystery:

> You withdraw and find
> Your head, too, is full,
> with raven wings beating.

One looks for explanations, but the opening poems caution readers about desiring reassuring stories. Contemporary healing is not so straightforward.

Recently, Hoffmann offered a personal context for the stories of book I:

> I was struggling to make sense of my cultural identity, attempting to piece
> together the bits and pieces I thought would give me clearer vision. Because
> of the disconnect to so many vital parts of those "bits and pieces," such as my
> father, history, place among my people, and so on, I wrote mainly from a place
> of anger and blame. . . .
> My epiphany came when I went back to Kake [the island village in Southeast
> Alaska where Hoffmann was born] and lived with my tribal uncle with whom
> I explained my perceptions, my struggles. He helped me arrive at clearer
> perceptions, and corrected many of my misunderstandings—about my father,
> about traditional ways of being.

With this explanation, we can read book I as the speaker's efforts to respond to the particular traumas that created a sense of alienation.

＊

Spiritual and cultural perceptions are shaped, though not determined, by changing material conditions. The present, often traumatic, context for *Raven's Echo* is not inherent to Tlingit life. The speaker's perceptions have developed in response to historical changes caused by the colonization of Tlingit people, which became more intrusive and destructive over time.

Although Spanish explorers came in 1779, it was the Russians and the Orthodox Church who had the first significant outside impact on Tlingit society. Yet they interfered little with traditional Tlingit practices. Major changes came in 1867 when Russia sold Alaska to the United States. Tlingit clans, the traditional centers of social and political power, argued that the land was not Russia's to sell and began to unite in resistance. For U.S. settlers and government, however, the rich natural resources of Southeast Alaska—gold, timber, and salmon—seemed irresistible. Hoffmann's home village of Kake was bombed and destroyed by the U.S. military in 1869 because of their resistance. Settler intrusions only increased. As commercial fishing developed, Southeast Alaska became the leading salmon producer in the world while the Tlingit people's catch could hardly sustain them. Cultural domination accompanied economic control. With the support of the government, Protestant missionaries sought to "civilize" the Native people by excluding Native languages, persecuting shamans, and legally segregating Native peoples. The effects were devastating.

In 1912, the Alaska Native Brotherhood (ANB) was established to resist racial discrimination. It focused on immediate political issues of fishing, hunting, and civil rights rather than cultural continuity. In its first few decades, the organization's influence gained for Native Alaskans the right to vote, receive workers' compensation, and attend public schools. At this time, out of necessity many Tlingit people were shifting away from subsistence living to wage work in canneries or commercial fishing near their traditional villages. Many moved into nuclear family houses in the major towns, relinquishing traditional extended family dwellings and selling their ceremonial objects to museums. In response to pressure from churches and government, Kake voted to cut down and burn their totem poles in the same year as the ANB's founding. Smallpox, influenza, and tuberculosis reduced the Tlingit population from approximately ten thousand in the 1700s to less than four thousand in 1920. This was a time of radical change.

Part of the impetus for cultural transformation was the Tlingit's newly increased integration into the U.S. political and economic system. In 1924, all Alaska Natives became enfranchised, and a number of Tlingit individuals were elected to the territorial legislature. A decade later a number of villages, including Kake, were incorporated, making members eligible for federal loans to purchase fishing boats and canneries. Traditional culture lost strength as federal governmental structures came to dominate economic and social life. Despite this, new Native organizations developed in response to declining Alaska Native land rights, and law suits were filed.

As a result of these suits as well as the needs of U.S. corporations, the Alaska Native Claims Settlement Act (ANCSA) became law in 1971. The act was a compromise among various interests. Alaska Natives needed to settle long standing, unresolved land claims, and corporations wanted to build the Prudhoe Bay pipeline. Following the failed efforts at tribal termination in the 1950s and 60s, a new Native policy was needed. Federal and state governments wanted to do this in a way that would engage Native groups in capitalist economic development and thereby reduce welfare and trusteeship obligations. ANCSA created thirteen Native regional and 205 village corporations, which received 44 million acres of land and nearly $1 billion.

ANCSA required a new Native leadership based on skills in business, economics, law, and politics rather than traditional wisdom. It considerably extended Native Alaskans' engagement in state and global economies. It also ended aboriginal titles to land and encouraged a short-term, profit-driven focus for resource management. Not surprisingly, ANCSA had little concern for cultural and spiritual values traditionally sustained in relation to the land. Yet ANCSA did prompt many individuals, as they enrolled in the corporations, to reengage their Native identity. And Native corporations did help foster a new sense of place through employment practices, investments, heritage programs, and other means. ANCSA clearly created a turning point for Native Alaskans; its impacts have been complex and variously understood.

In the midst of these socioeconomic structural changes, Tlingit people have been striving for cultural revitalization. The two books of *Raven's Echo* register the disjunctures and continuities between traditional and contemporary Tlingit life. As the speaker of "Saginaw Bay" explains, "I keep trying to see my life / against all this history," and thus concludes,

> [. . .] I might write a book.
> In it, I would tell how we all are pulled
> so many directions,
> how our lives are fragmented
> with so many gaps.

*

In response to these historical and contemporary traumas, Hoffmann states, "I believe there comes a point where one must name and own who and what he is in order to take responsibility for where his actions and attitudes are coming from." Book 2, "Reconstruction," presents neo-traditionalist ways of integrating traditional culture into contemporary life. The concluding poem, "Reconstruction," is the culmination of these efforts.

The poem's speaker often feels alienated from traditional life yet yearns to make experiential connections to it. The significance of the land, subsistence fishing, warrior identity, and the role of elders in maintaining historical memory are woven into the poem. The opening stanza calls attention to experiential uncertainties related to these themes. It begins, "I thought my life was in layers." Uneasiness about this lack of integration is reinforced by the stanza's last line, "I always heard we live in two worlds," implying that commonly held frameworks for understanding need reconsideration. The "living in two worlds" trope cannot adequately capture the speaker's efforts to understand his contemporary Tlingit experience, but neither do easy assumptions about connections to place and land.

The following stanzas of "Reconstruction" take up this central issue of land. The tone of irony in the phrase "feed us like mother with milk" sets up the sense of alienation that follows: "I never hunted, could not speak the language of the forest." The speaker addresses this common dilemma of Native urbanization and rural change by listing vague details which reduce the landscape to its cursory material components: "mudflats here, cliffs there, clouds above." We can see the speaker's limitations by comparing his list to a description given by Kake elder Fred Friday, quoted in Thomas F. Thornton's *Being and Place among the Tlingit*: "The Native people know all the points and rocks and every little area by name. . . . These areas were used so much that we were familiar with every little place." Friday's form of attention is part of everyday subsistence living; the speaker's description lacks that personal engagement: "But for all the details / it could not come to life. . . . / I puzzled over this." He does not yet know how to see.

In present day Southeast Alaska, one aspect of revitalization is a renewed emphasis on subsistence living. Fishing, hunting, and gathering had traditionally sustained Tlingit people, and continue to sustain up to one-third of village households. For many more, however, subsistence living continues symbolically. The speaker experiences this during a fishing excursion: "We pulled in fat halibut. There was so much! / We thought we fished good!" The exclamation marks suggest ironic surprise and mark the fishermen as outsiders. Uncle Topsy offers the speaker an alternative perspective, one might say a foundational approach, applicable to both symbolic and economic subsistence practices. "But the fish came to us," he states, implying that this fishing expedition is both a material and spiritual venture.

Revitalization does not come easily; nor is it without social complications. The tension between subsistence as identity and subsistence as a means of making a living is shaped by contemporary socioeconomic structures. Native corporations created through ANCSA have made subsistence increasingly difficult, dangerous, and unproductive through their land management practices, including extensive clear cutting of forests. Corporations need to make a profit, and timber is a significant source of revenue. Subsistence living is economically marginal. Those relying on it are often the first to leave villages. Embedded in the speaker's puzzle are questions of economic and social justice within villages. Sustaining traditions symbolically does not necessarily help maintain those who practice subsistence as a living.

After exploring Tlingit identity in connection to land and subsistence, "Reconstruction" then works through another form of Native identity, "being a warrior." This tried on identity, "Trained myself to be angry," seems out of place when the speaker looks at his much admired uncle with his oxygen tank and tubes. Again, Uncle Topsy offers a different model for being Tlingit, one that is less about direct political resistance and more focused on self and cultural reflection. "He put his hand on my heart / . . . / It will all come to you, if you stop fighting so hard." In his introduction to Tlingit culture, Wallace Olson notes that one of the losses the people have experienced is that they no longer send their sons to live with and be taught by their uncles. This process of learning is part of what the speaker recreates and the poet himself experienced.

Just as these poems complicate the topics of subsistence living and the warrior identity, so too do they complicate the role of elders. While *Raven's Echo* recognizes the importance of elders, "Reconstruction" cautions against idealizing and thus ossifying them. "I thought I needed his memories, his life," the speaker states. "But we are more than our pasts," Hoffmann has noted elsewhere. Uncle Topsy tells the speaker, "You know, even when you know the answers, listen. Just listen."

This form of listening is the work of neo-traditionalists like Hoffmann: heeding both past and present. The past cannot be recreated, even if the speaker "wanted it to come back." Yet the past must be meaningfully engaged: "I would have to design the dance staff to tell our story," one that is "connected, not disjointed." Old photographs and tapes of traditional music now become part of his reconstruction project. The past and the present, the material and the spiritual, all finally come together. He is learning Uncle Topsy's lesson, already stated but repeated as the last lines of "Reconstruction" and *Raven's Echo* as a whole:

> [. . .] "You just have to listen, nephew.
> It will all come to you, if you stop fighting so hard. It will."

In "Reconstruction," Raven dances in mythic time, and Kake dancers' rearticulations take place in present time. Hoffmann is not naïve about economic, political, and social conflicts between Native peoples and the dominant society. Language, land rights, social structures, ownership of cultural objects (*at.oow*), and many more points of conflict do matter. Yet he asserts that we are not sole agents of our lives and cultures. By listening, one can again recognize that "the fish came to us" and that it was Uncle Topsy who "was bringing us here, home," not vice versa. By listening, Hoffmann's poetry finds the ultimate goal: the way to be human.

✳

In 1912 Robert Davis Hoffmann's home village of Kake became the first Alaskan village to be recognized as a municipality, and thus it adopted the use of English and Western law. The same year, a new cannery opened, offering both economic opportunities and liabilities. One hundred years later, the Keex' Kwaan Dancers performed at the Kake Centennial Celebration to commemorate that decision. Magistrate Mike Jackson explained that "becoming a municipality meant that traditional ways would need to be changed in order to prepare children for new forms of work and social structure." Yet, Jackson concluded, "We're still here. . . . People in this community choose to stay to put a face to the land." But what this means is complicated as today's Kake leaders focus on economic development and cultural revitalization. These goals do not easily or simply fit together as Kake is both a Tlingit village and a Native corporation. Land and culture can mean something quite different within the two contexts.

Contemporary dance groups like Keex' Kwaan reflect a shift in material and spiritual authority within villages. Although songs are still clan property and permission must be granted for a dance group to perform one, the dance groups themselves are community based, with members from various clans and even non-Natives participating. Elders have expressed concern, Nora (Marks) and Richard Dauenhauer explain, "lest the spirits evoked by the young people wander aimlessly, floating in space unanswered, unattended." Most culture group members and most villagers are Christian. Kake has six Christian churches. Some are clearly supportive of Tlingit cultural revitalization. Others, particularly Pentecostals, stand against it. And both positions are complexly economic, social, political, and religious.

Listening within this conflicted context of Native Southeastern Alaska is not easy, as *Raven's Echo* makes clear. Economic complexities and inequalities, the range of meanings for subsistence activities, the challenge of Kake being among the most industrialized Native villages, conflicting interpretations of recent and mythical pasts, the variety of religious practices, and other conditions must be recognized, listened to, and reckoned with as part of the continuous struggle to reconstruct Native, specifically Tlingit, ways of being human, these poems suggest. Hoffmann offers us an "ethnography of a problem," but more than that, he presents a poetic and experiential report of ways to address this problem in personal, material, and spiritual ways.

We too must discover and create ways of being responsible for what we experience through our reading of *Raven's Echo*.

ABOUT THE AUTHOR

ROBERT DAVIS HOFFMANN imagines the mythical and historical life of his Tlingit people. He addresses historical and cultural loss, and writes about the complications of identity that result from growing up in two cultures and being half-native, ultimately moving toward catharsis and integrity. He now enjoys retirement in Sitka, Alaska where makes his artwork and helps his wife, Kris with her fantastical garden. His latest work is *Village Boy: Poems of Cultural Identity*.